Essential Audition Songs

male & female Vocalists — love songs

	page no.	on the CD	vocal range
Amazed — Lonestar	2	Track 1	
Embraceable You — Ella Fitzgerald	8	Track 2	
The First Time Ever I Saw Your Face — Roberta Flack	13	Track 3	
Get Here — Oleta Adams	16	Track 4	
I Turn To You — Christina Aguilera	24	Track 6	
Kiss Me — Sixpence None The Richer	30	Track 7	
Let's Stay Together — Al Green	21	Track 5	
Save The Best For Last — Vanessa Williams	34	Track 8	
Saving All My Love For You — Whitney Houston	40	Track 9	
You Don't Have To Say You Love Me — Dusty Springfield	45	Track 10	

International MUSIC Publications

© International Music Publications Limited
Griffin House 161 Hammersmith Road London W6 8BS England

Editorial, Production and Recording: Artemis Music Limited
Design and Production: Space DPS Limited

Published 2003

RESPECT THE VALUE OF MUSIC

Reproducing this music in any form is illegal and forbidden by the Copyright, Designs and Patents Act 1988

Amazed

Words and Music by Marv Green,
Aimee Mayo and Chris Lindsey

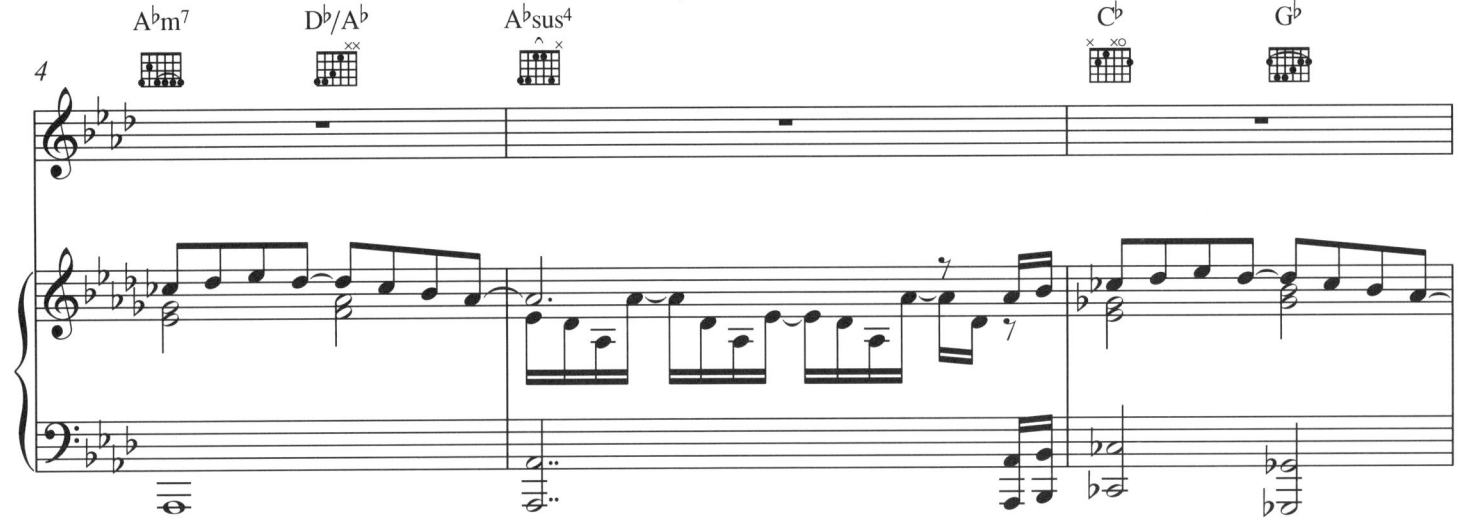

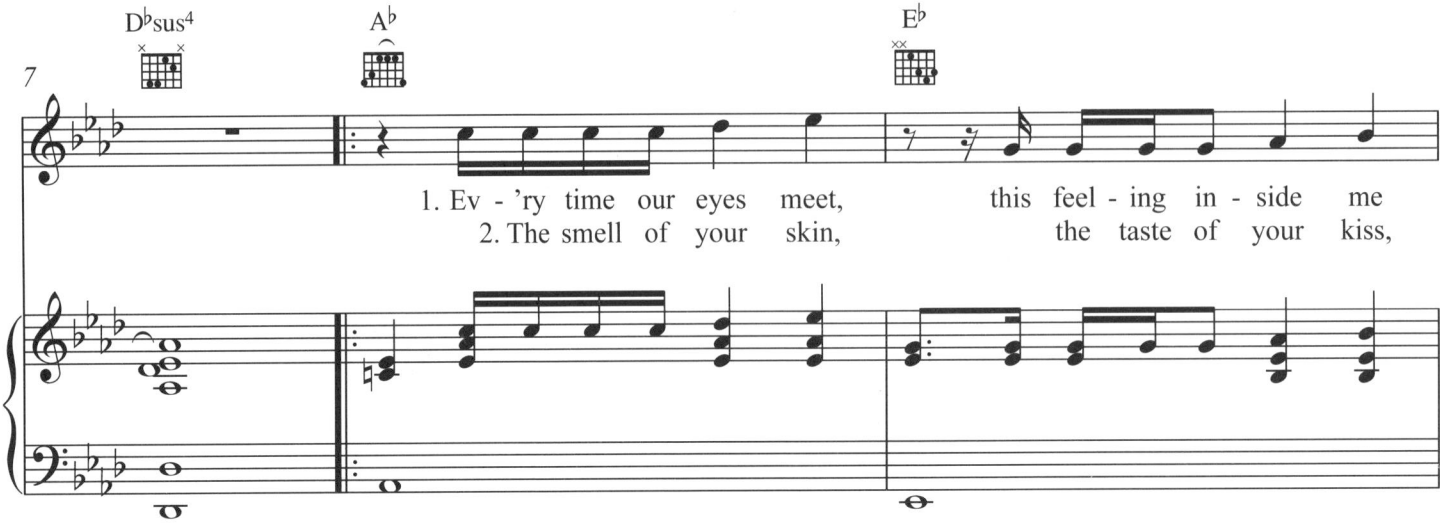

1. Ev-'ry time our eyes meet, this feel-ing in-side me
2. The smell of your skin, the taste of your kiss,

© 1993 Gold Wheat Music, Careers BMG Music Publishing Inc and Songs of Dreamworks, USA
Warner/Chappell Music Ltd, London W6 8BS, BMG Music Publishing Ltd, London SW6 3JW
and Cherry Lane Music Publishing, USA

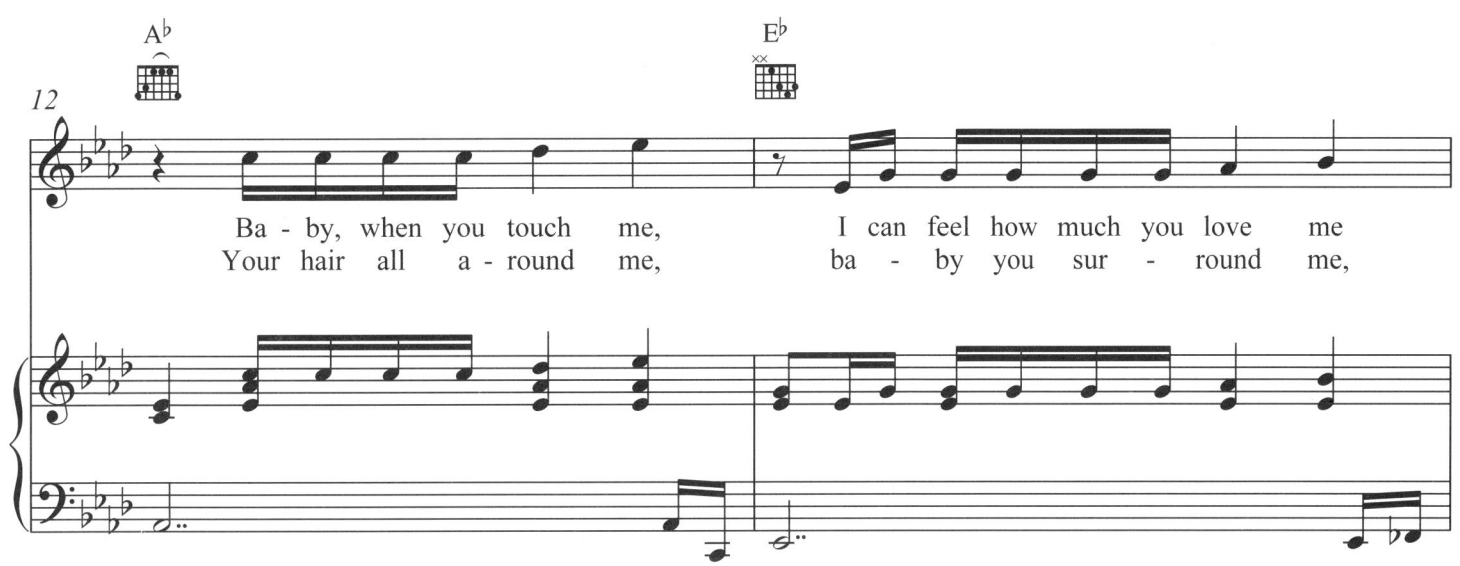

INTRODUCTION & WELCOME

BREATHING

WARM UP G MAJOR SCALE TO C MAJOR SCALE

THIS GROOVE TECHNICAL EXERCISE

WATER COME A MY EYE

KUMBAYA   PAGE 59   CD2 TRACK 9 – 13
                                          4 PART HARMONY

YOU AND ME BACKING VOCALS
ROCKSCHOOL COMPANION
                                GUIDE

AUTUMN LEAVES

WHAT IS LOVE?

FLY ME TO THE MOON

WEEK 4 WIDNES
WEEK 3 RUNCORN

F   C
Food Glorious Food

F	F+	F6	F7
F	F+	F6	Am
Bb	Am	F7	Bb
Am	C/G		

Grade 1 *Technical Exercises*

In this section, the examiner will ask you to perform the four exercises printed below. You do not memorise the exercises (and you may use the book in the exam) but the examiner will be looking for t and confidence of your response. The examiner will also give you credit for the level of your musicality.

Exercise 1: Rhythm   Disc 1

You will be asked to perform the exercise below as written to a backing track accompaniment in th A short sound check will be given.

Exercise 2: Scales   Disc 1

You will be asked to perform a major scale in the following rhythms to a backing track accompanime exam. You will be allowed to choose your own starting note between **A-E** which will be played to you be begin. You will be asked a selection by the examiner and you will perform the exercise *legato* to a soun own choosing.

Embraceable You

Words and Lyrics by George Gershwin
and Ira Gershwin

Doz - ens of girls would storm_ up;
I went a - bout re - cit - ing,
I had to lock my door. Some - how I could - n't warm_ up to
Here's one who'll nev - er fall! But I'm a - fraid the writ - ing is
one be - fore. What was it that con - trolled_ me?
on the wall. My nose I used to turn_ up

© 1930 (renewed) WB Music Corp, USA
Warner/Chappell Music Ltd, London W6 8BS

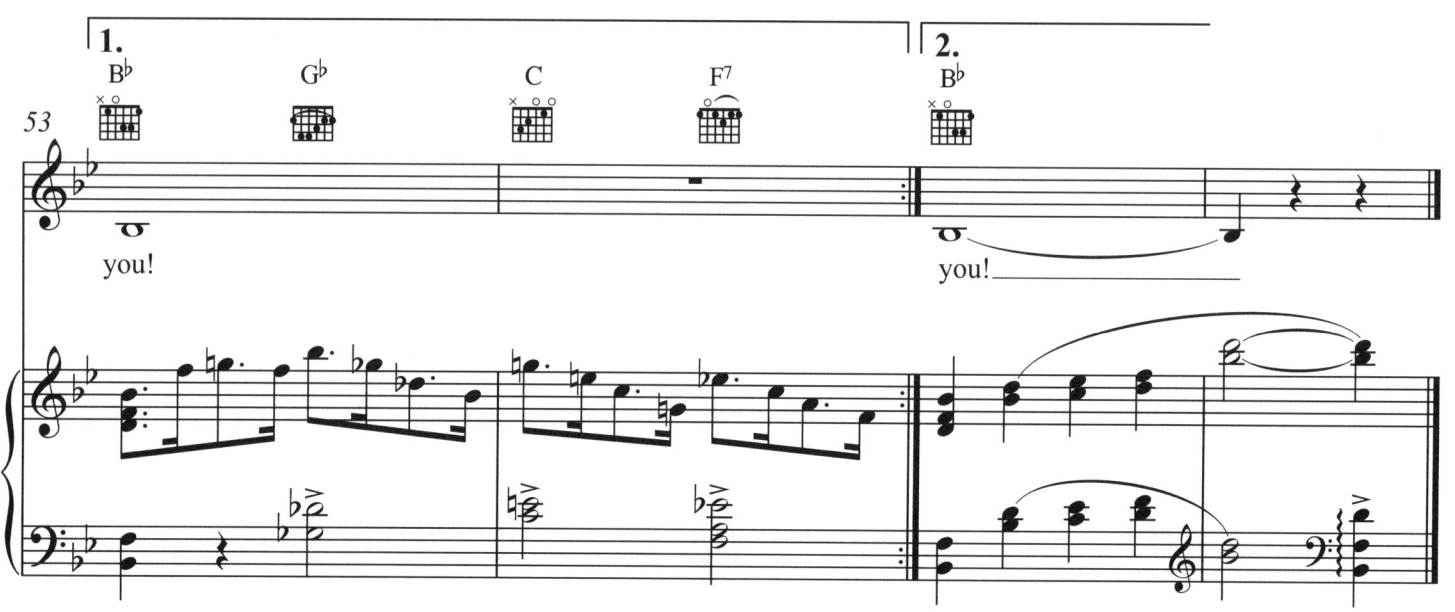

The First Time Ever I Saw Your Face

Backing

Words and Music by
Ewan MacColl

♩=60

1. The first time ever I saw your face,
2. And the first time ever I kissed your mouth,

(Verse 3 see block lyric)

I thought the sun rose in your eyes.
I felt the earth move in my hand,

© 1962 Stormking Music Inc, USA
Harmony Music Ltd, London W8 7TQ

Verse 3:
And the first time ever I lay with you
I felt your heart so close to mine
And I knew our joy would fill the earth
And last till the end of time my love
And it would last till the end of time my love.

Get Here

Words and Music by Brenda Russell

Slowly

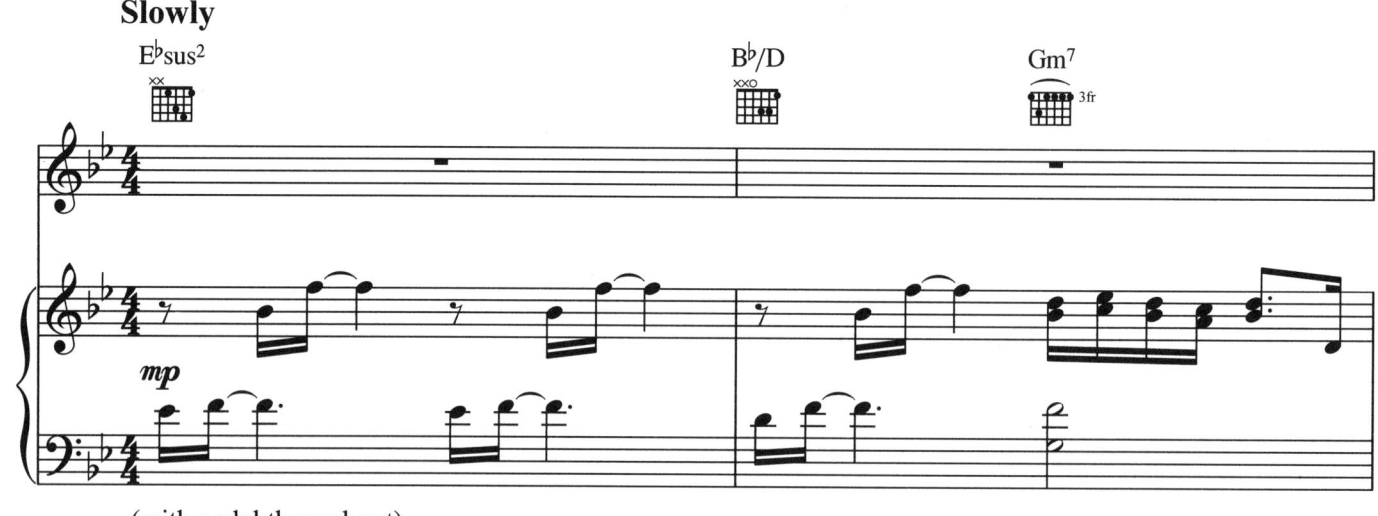

(with pedal throughout)

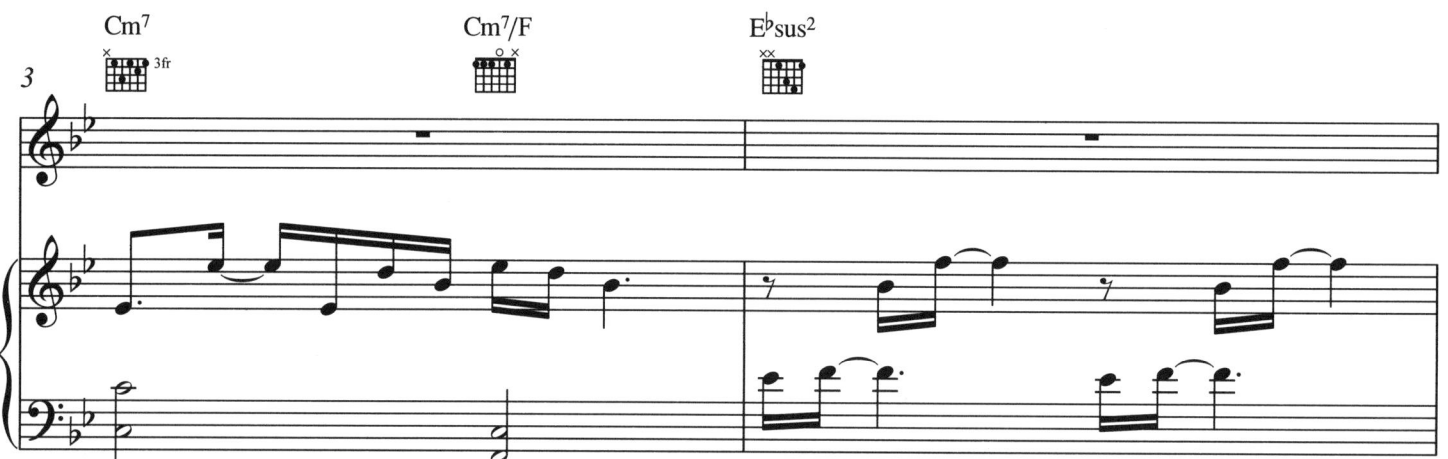

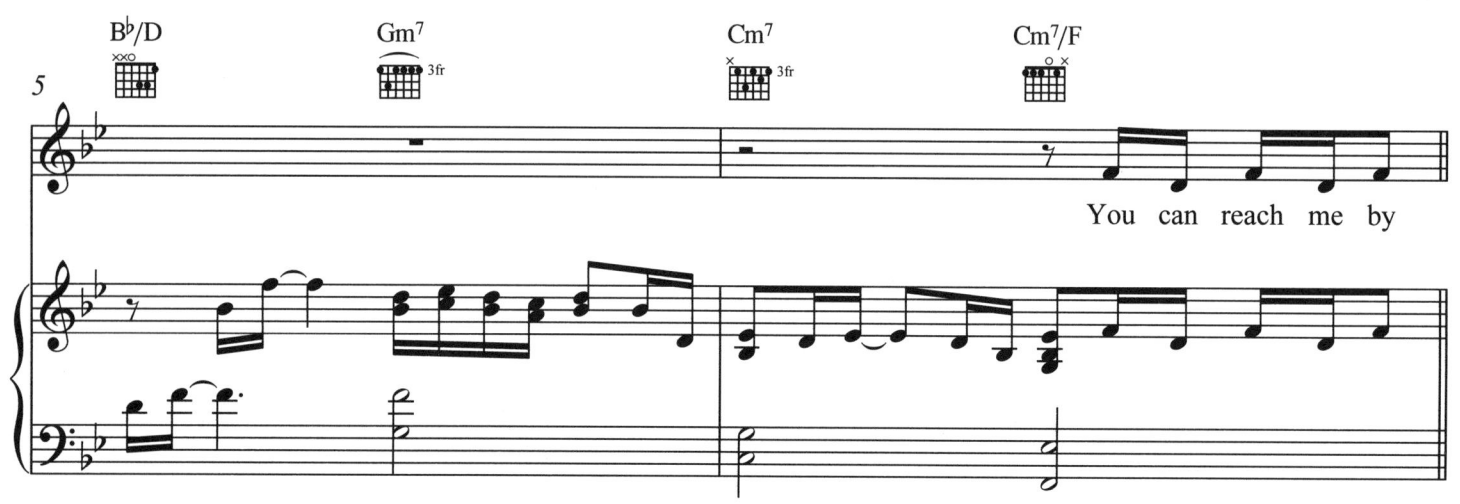

You can reach me by

© 1986 Rutland Road Music, USA
Warner/Chappell Music Ltd, London W6 8BS

Let's Stay Together

Backing

Words and Music by Al Jackson Jr,
Al Green and Willie Mitchell

Medium pop tempo

1. I'm, I'm so in love with you
2. Since, since we've been to-geth-er
3. Why, why peo-ple break up,

what-ev-er you want to do is all right with
lov-ing you for ev - er is what I
turn a-round and make up I just can't

© 1962 Jec Music Publishing Co and Al Green Music Inc, USA
Burlington Music Co Ltd, London W6 8BS and Rondor Music (London) Ltd, London W6 8JA

I Turn To You

Backing

Words and Music by Diane Warren

Slowly ♩ = 76

1. When I'm lost in the rain,
   in your eyes I know I'll find the light to light my way.
   When I'm scared,

2. the will to win, I just reach for you and I can reach the sky again.
   I can do

© 1997 Realsongs, USA
EMI Music Publishing Ltd, London WC2H 0QY

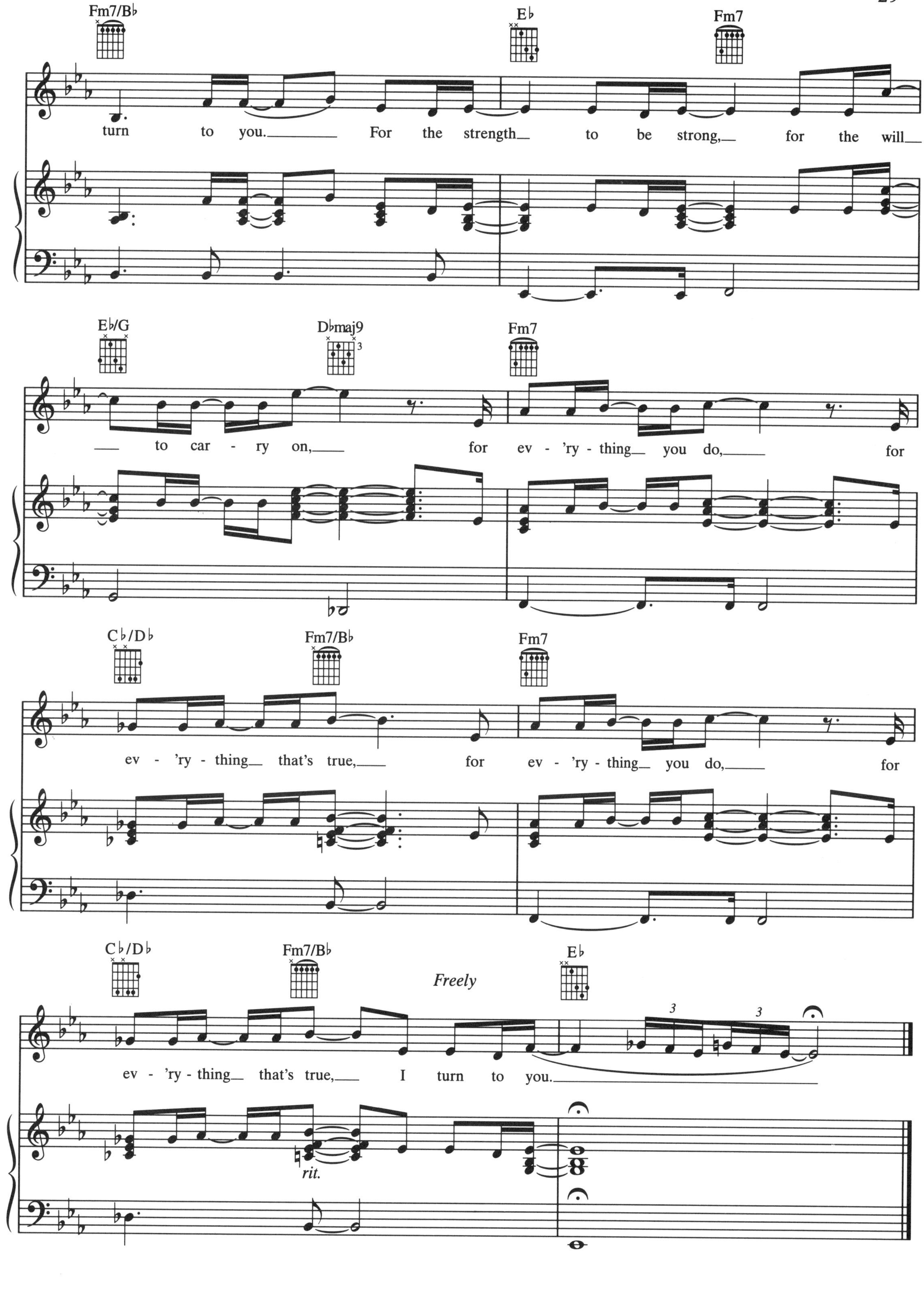
Fm7/B♭
E♭
Fm7
turn to you. For the strength to be strong, for the will
E♭/G
D♭maj9
Fm7
to car - ry on, for ev - 'ry - thing you do, for
C♭/D♭
Fm7/B♭
Fm7
ev - 'ry - thing that's true, for ev - 'ry - thing you do, for
C♭/D♭
Fm7/B♭
Freely
E♭
ev - 'ry - thing that's true, I turn to you.
rit.

Kiss Me

Words and Music by Matt Slocum

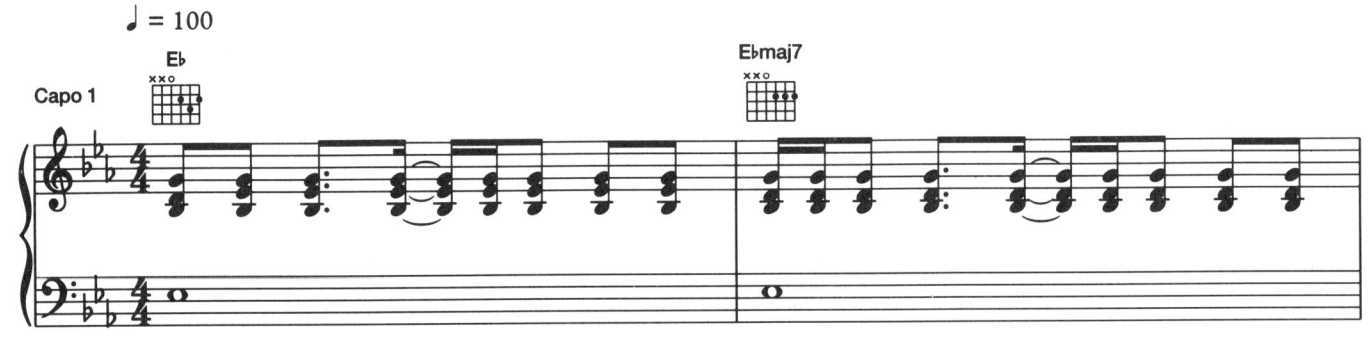

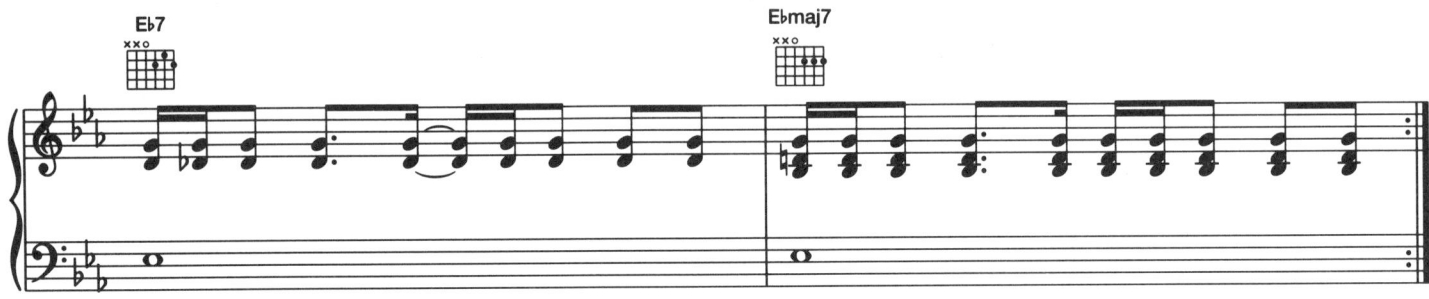

Kiss___ me, out of the bearded barley___
Kiss___ me down by the broken tree house,___

___ nightly, beside the green, green grass,
___ swing___ me upon its hanging tire,___

© 1999 My So Called Music and Squint Songs, USA
Warner/Chappell Music Ltd, London W6 8BS

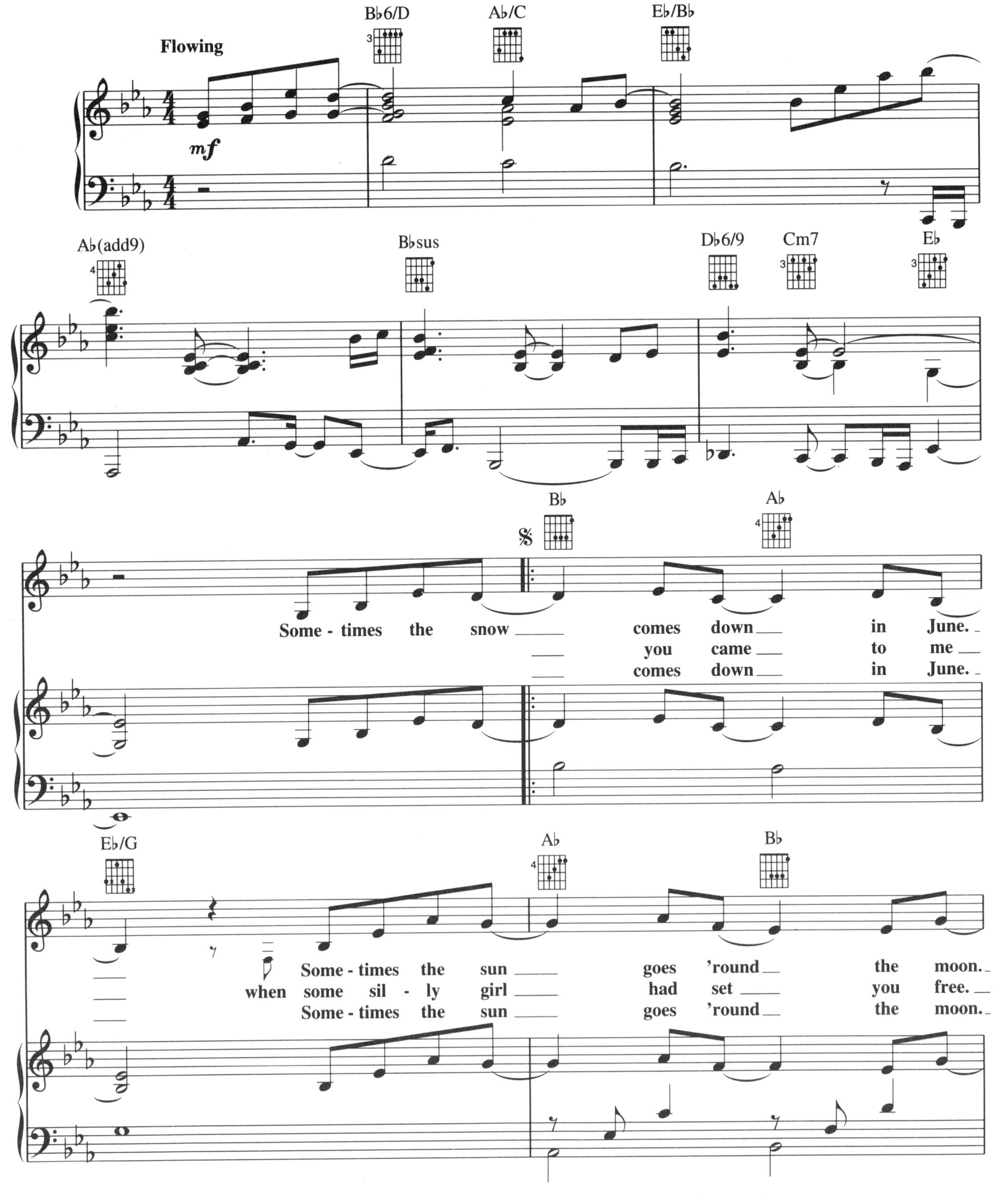

38

Saving All My Love For You

Words by Gerry Goffin
Music by Michael Masser

© 1978 Screen Gems-EMI Music Inc, Lauren Wesley Music and Prince Street Music, USA
SCreen Gems-EMI Music Ltd, London WC2H 0QY, Universal/MCA Music Ltd, London W6 8JA and Copyright Control

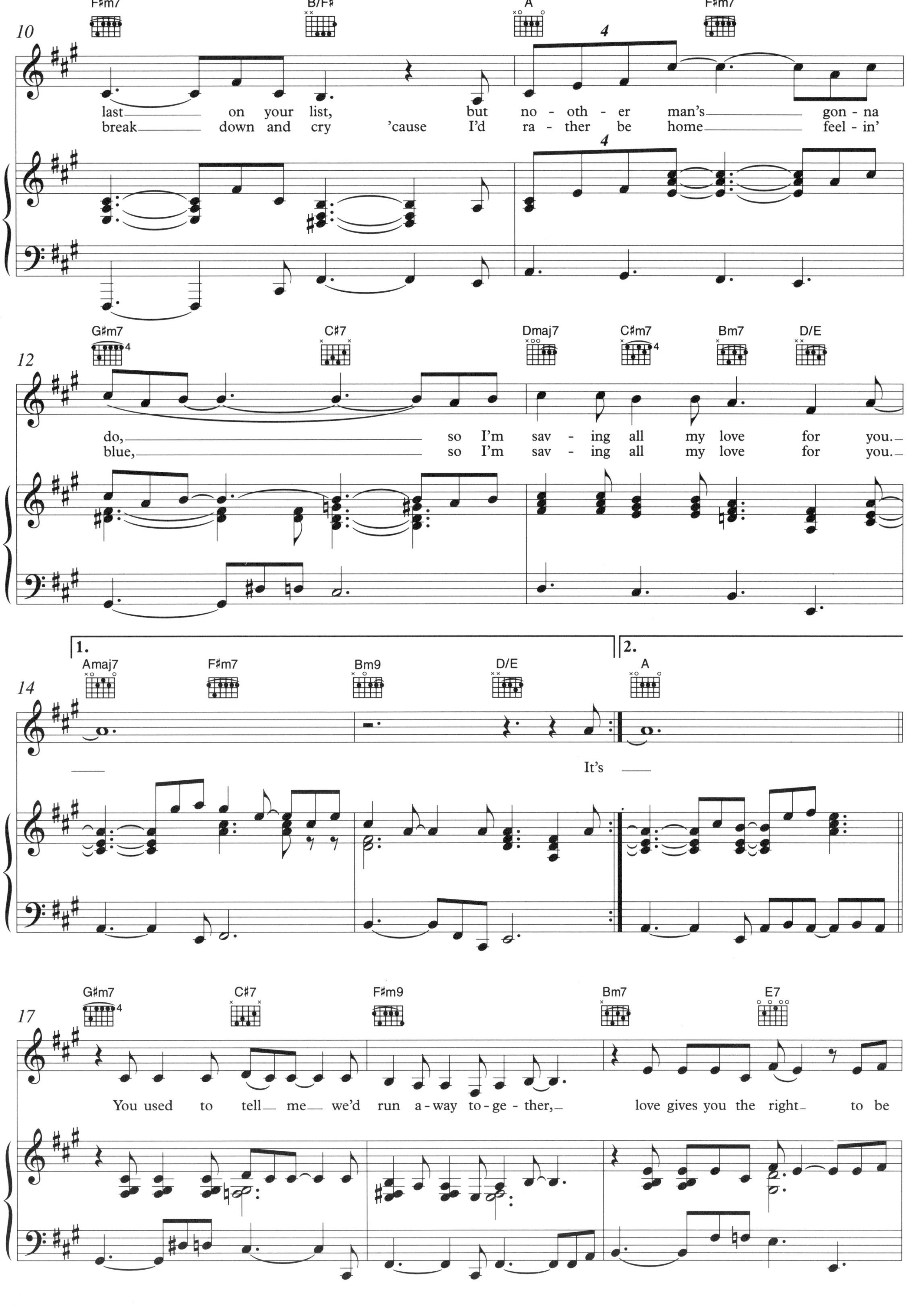
F♯m7
B/F♯
A
F♯m7
10
last on your list, but no-oth-er man's gon-na
break down and cry 'cause I'd ra-ther be home feel-in'
G♯m7
C♯7
Dmaj7
C♯m7
Bm7
D/E
12
do, so I'm sav-ing all my love for you.
blue, so I'm sav-ing all my love for you.
1.
2.
Amaj7
F♯m7
Bm9
D/E
A
14
It's
G♯m7
C♯7
F♯m9
Bm7
E7
17
You used to tell me we'd run a-way to-ge-ther, love gives you the right to be

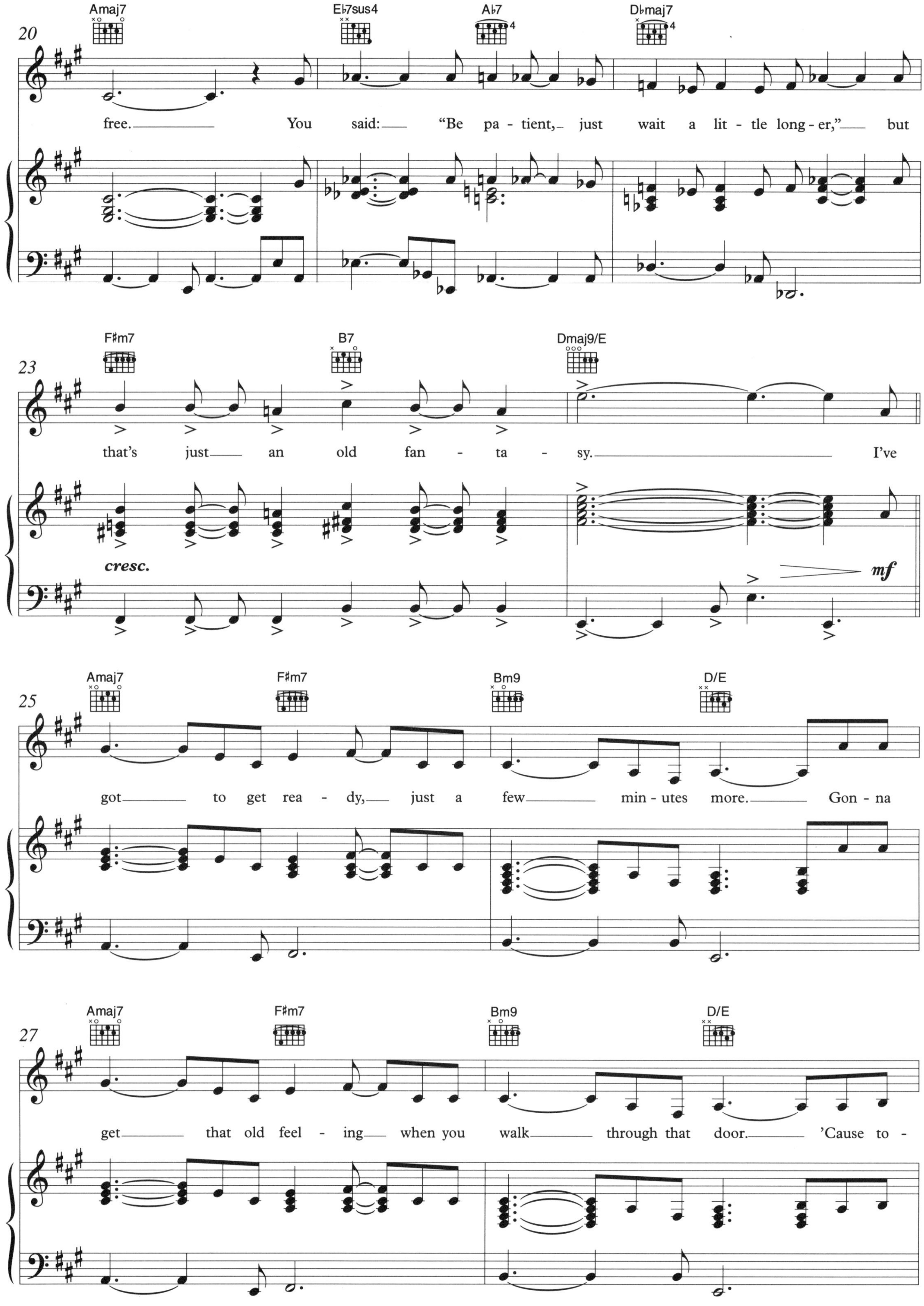
20
Amaj7
E♭7sus4
A♭7
D♭maj7
free. You said: "Be pa - tient, just wait a lit - tle long - er," but
23
F♯m7
B7
Dmaj9/E
that's just an old fan - ta - sy. I've
cresc.
mf
25
Amaj7
F♯m7
Bm9
D/E
got to get rea - dy, just a few min - utes more. Gon - na
27
Amaj7
F♯m7
Bm9
D/E
get that old feel - ing when you walk through that door. 'Cause to -

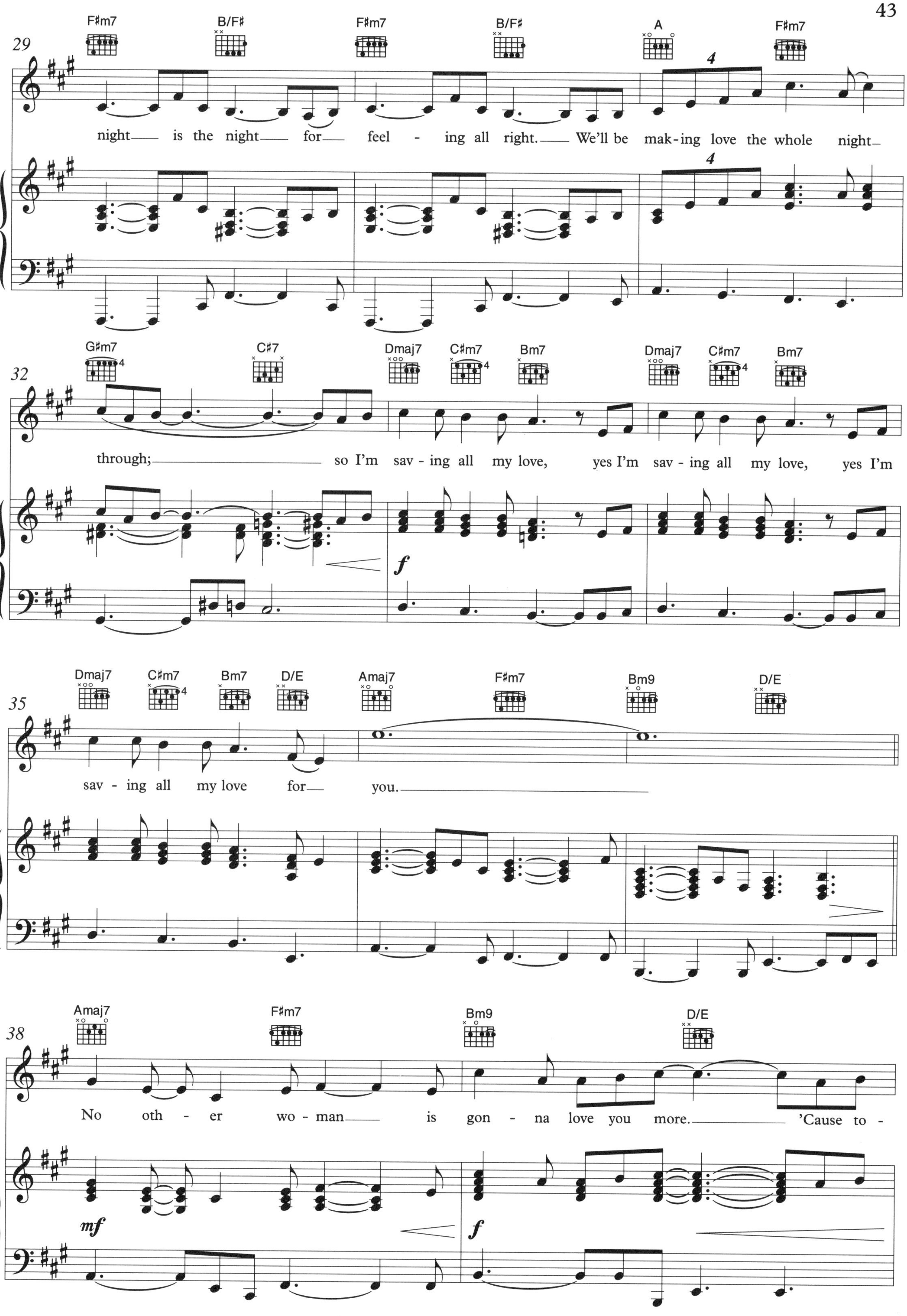
29
F♯m7 B/F♯ F♯m7 B/F♯ A F♯m7
night is the night for feel - ing all right. We'll be mak-ing love the whole night
32
G♯m7 C♯7 Dmaj7 C♯m7 Bm7 Dmaj7 C♯m7 Bm7
through; so I'm sav - ing all my love, yes I'm sav - ing all my love, yes I'm
35
Dmaj7 C♯m7 Bm7 D/E Amaj7 F♯m7 Bm9 D/E
sav - ing all my love for you.
38
Amaj7 F♯m7 Bm9 D/E
No oth - er wo - man is gon - na love you more. 'Cause to -
mf
f

Track 10
Backing

You Don't Have To Say You Love Me

Original Words by Vito Pallavicini
English Words by Simon Napier-Bell and Vicki Wickham
Music by Pino Donaggio

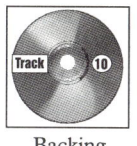

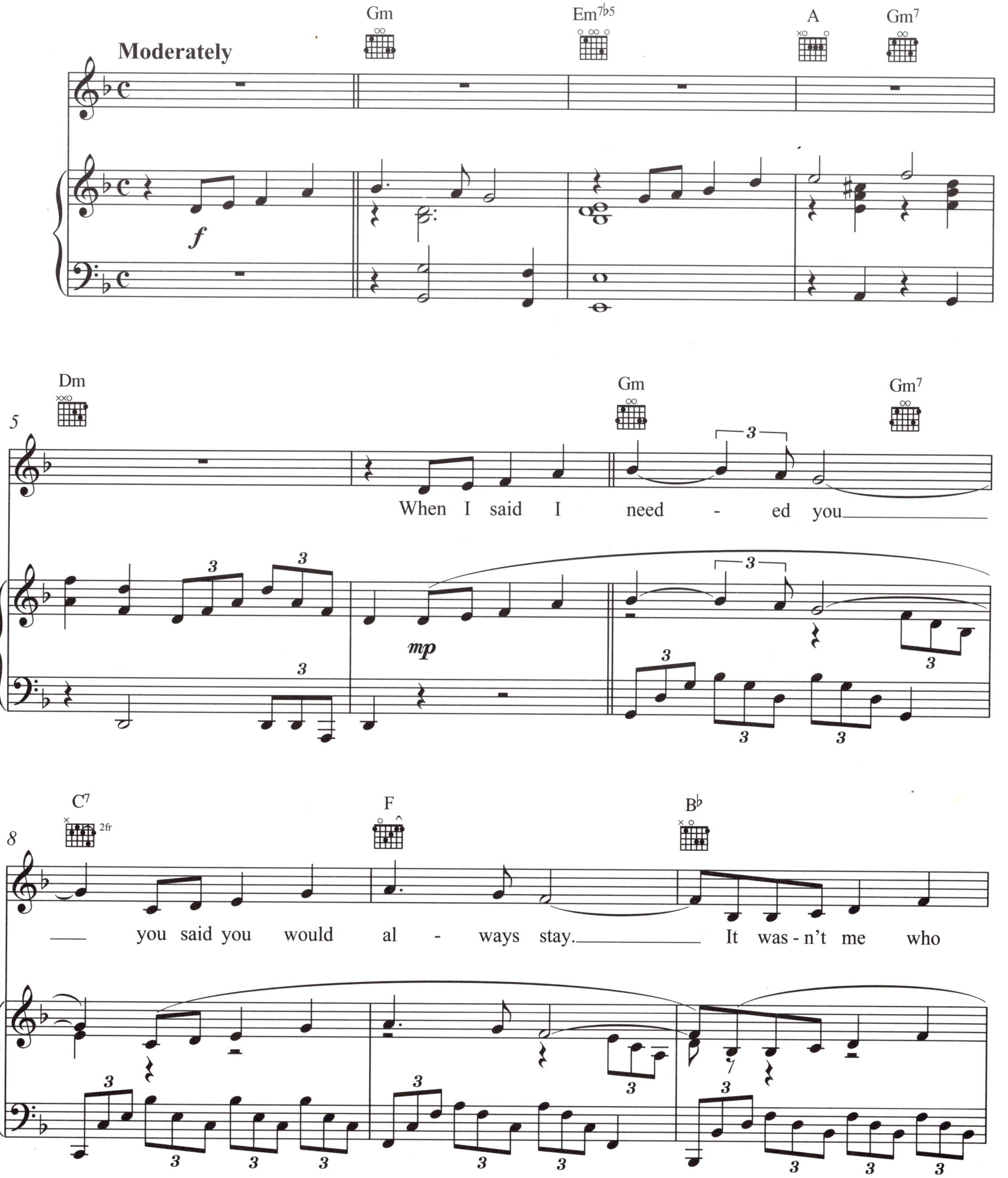

Karaoke Classics
9696A   PVG/CD   ISBN: 1-84328-202-X

Back For Good - Delilah - Hey Baby - I Will Always Love You - I Will Survive - Let Me Entertain You - Reach - New York, New York - Summer Nights - Wild Thing

Party Hits
9499A   PVG/CD   ISBN: 1-84328-097-8

Come On Eileen - Dancing Queen - Groove Is In The Heart - Hi Ho Silver Lining - Holiday - House Of Fun - The Loco-Motion - Love Shack - Staying Alive - Walking On Sunshine

Disco
9493A   PVG/CD   ISBN: 1-84328-091-4

I Feel Love - I Will Survive - I'm So Excited - Lady Marmalade - Le Freak - Never Can Say Goodbye - On The Radio - Relight My - Fire - YMCA - You Sexy Thing

Celebration Songs
9733A   PVG/CD   ISBN: 1-84328-241-0

Anniversary Waltz - Auld Lang Syne – Celebration – Congratulations - God Save The Queen - Happy Birthday - Happy Birthday To You - My Way - The Best - We Are The Champions

YOU'RE THE VOICE

8861A PV/CD

Casta Diva from Norma - Vissi D'arte from Tosca - Un Bel Di Vedremo from Madam Butterfly - Addio, Del Passato from La Traviata - J'ai Perdu Mon Eurydice from Orphee Et Eurydice - Les Tringles Des Sistres Tintaient from Carmen - Porgi Amor from Le Nozze Di Figaro - Ave Maria from Otello

8860A PVG/CD

Delilah - Green Green Grass Of Home - Help Yourself - I'll Never Fall In Love Again - It's Not Unusual - Mama Told Me Not To Come - Sexbomb - Thunderball - What's New Pussycat - You Can Leave Your Hat On

9297A PVG/CD

Beauty And The Beast - Because You Loved Me - Falling Into You - The First Time Ever I Saw Your Face - It's All Coming Back To Me Now - Misled - My Heart Will Go On - The Power Of Love - Think Twice - When I Fall In Love

9349A PVG/CD

Chain Of Fools - A Deeper Love - Do Right Woman, Do Right Man - I Knew You Were Waiting (For Me) - I Never Loved A Man (The Way I Loved You) - I Say A Little Prayer - Respect - Think - Who's Zooming Who - (You Make Me Feel Like) A Natural Woman

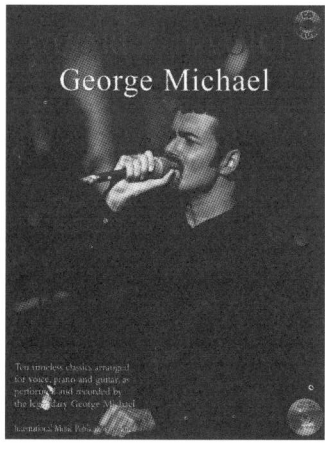

9007A PVG/CD

Careless Whisper - A Different Corner - Faith - Father Figure - Freedom '90 - I'm Your Man - I Knew You Were Waiting (For Me) - Jesus To A Child - Older - Outside

9606A PVG/CD

Don't Let Me Be Misunderstood - Feeling Good - I Loves You Porgy - I Put A Spell On You - Love Me Or Leave Me - Mood Indigo - My Baby Just Cares For Me - Ne Me Quitte Pas (If You Go Away) - Nobody Knows You When You're Down And Out - Take Me To The Water

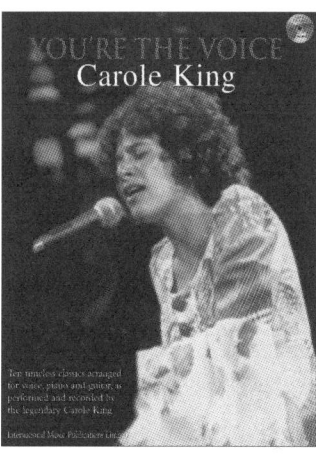

9700A PVG/CD

Beautiful - Crying In The Rain - I Feel The Earth Move - It's Too Late - (You Make Me Feel Like) A Natural Woman - So Far Away - Way Over Yonder - Where You Lead - Will You Love Me Tomorrow - You've Got A Friend

9746A PVG/CD

April In Paris - Come Rain Or Come Shine - Fly Me To The Moon (In Other Words) - I've Got You Under My Skin - The Lady Is A Tramp - My Kinda Town (Chicago Is) - My Way - Theme From *New York, New York* - Someone To Watch Over Me - Something Stupid

9770A PVG/CD

Cry Me A River - Evergreen (A Star Is Born) - Happy Days Are Here Again - I've Dreamed Of You - Memory - My Heart Belongs To Me - On A Clear Day (You Can See Forever) - Someday My Prince Will Come - Tell Him (duet with Celine Dion) - The Way We Were

9799A PVG/CD

Boogie Woogie Bugle Boy - Chapel Of Love - Friends - From A Distance - Hello In There - One For My Baby (And One More For The Road) - Only In Miami - The Rose - When A Man Loves A Woman - Wind Beneath My Wings

The outstanding vocal series from IMP

CD contains full backings for each song,
professionally arranged to recreate the sounds of the original recording

    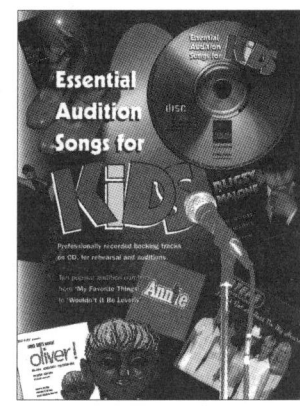

ESSENTIAL AUDITION SONGS FOR FEMALE VOCALISTS

Broadway
7171A   Book and CD   ISBN: 1859098010
Anything Goes - As Long As He Needs Me - Being Alive - But Not For Me - Fifty Percent - Johnny One Note - Nothing - People - Take Me Or Leave Me - There Won't Be Trumpets

Jazz Standards
7021A   Book and CD   ISBN: 1859097529
Cry Me A River - Desafinado - Ev'ry Time We Say Goodbye - Fever - It's Only A Paper Moon - Mad About The Boy - My Baby Just Cares For Me - Stormy Weather (Keeps Rainin' All The Time) - Summertime - They Can't Take That Away From Me

Pop Ballads
6939A   Book and CD   ISBN: 185909712X
Anything For You - Do You Know Where You're Going To - I Will Always Love You - Killing Me Softly With His - My Heart Will Go On - Over The Rainbow - Promise Me - The Greatest Love Of All - The Way We Were - Walk On By

Pop Divas
7769A   Book and CD   ISBN: 1859099874
Beautiful Stranger - Believe - Genie In A Bottle - I Don't Want To Wait - I Try - Pure Shores - The Greatest Love Of All - Un-Break My Heart - Waiting For Tonight - Without You

ESSENTIAL AUDITION SONGS FOR MALE VOCALISTS

Broadway
9185A   Book and CD   ISBN: 1843280124
Don't Get Around Much Anymore - From Sophisticated Ladies - Get Me To The Church On Time From My Fair Lady - If I Were A Rich Man From Fiddler On The Roof - It Don't Mean A Thing (If It Ain't Got That Swing) From Sophisticated Ladies - It's All Right With Me From Can-Can - On The Street Where You Live From My Fair Lady - Thank Heaven For Little Girls From Gigi - The Lady Is A Tramp From Babes In Arms - Wandrin' Star From Paint Your Wagon - With A Little Bit Of Luck From My Fair Lady

Crooners
9495A   Book and CD   ISBN: 1843280922
Can't Take My Eyes Off You - I Left My Heart In San Francisco - Mack The Knife - My Way - Swingin' On A Star - The Way We Were - Theme From 'New York, New York' - (What A) Wonderful World - When I Fall In Love - Volare

ESSENTIAL AUDITION SONGS FOR FEMALE & MALE VOCALISTS

Duets
7432A   Book and CD   ISBN: 1859099009
Barcelona - Don't Go Breaking My Heart - Endless Love - I Got You Babe - I Knew You Were Waiting (For Me) - (I've Had) The Time Of My Life - It Takes Two - Kids - Nothing's Gonna Stop Us Now - Summer Nights

Essential Audition Songs For Kids
7341A   Book and CD   ISBN: 1859098673
Bugsy Malone - Consider Yourself Love's Got A Hold On My Heart Maybe This Time - My Favourite Things - My Name Is Tallulah The Rainbow - We're In The Money Wouldn't It Be Loverly - You're Fully Dressed Without A Smile

Essential Audition Songs For Wannabe Pop Stars
9735A   Book and CD   ISBN: 1843282453
Angels - Anything Is Possible - Back For Good - Ev'ry Time We Say Goodbye - Flying Without Wings - Genie In A Bottle - Get Happy - Reach - Up On The Roof - Whole Again